The Burden Lifters

DATE DUE			

Books by Michael Waters

The Burden Lifters (1989)
Anniversary of the Air (1985)
Not Just Any Death (1979)
Fish Light (1975)

*Dissolve to Island: On the Poetry
    of John Logan* (Ed.) 1984

The
Burden
Lifters

Michael Waters

Carnegie Mellon University Press
Pittsburgh 1989

Acknowledgments

811.54
W316
145908
Feb. 1989

Chiaroscuro: "Vespers"
Crazyhorse: "The Burden Lifters"
5 AM: "Deadly Nightshade," "Traffic Island"
The Georgia Review: "Morpho"
Indiana Review: "Toward a Definition of Desire"
Ironwood: "Horse," "Small Song," "Foundling," "Keats' Lips,"
   "The Turtles of Santa Rosa"
Memphis State Review: "Brooklyn Waterfall," "Umbrellas with Souls,"
   "Well Water"
The Missouri Review: "Snakes"
The North American Review: "Yellow Stars"
The Ohio Review: "Lipstick"
Poetry: "Reading Dickens," "The Conversion of Saint Paul,"
   "Romance in the Old Folks' Home"
Quarterly West: "The Lighthouse Keeper at Sparrow Point"
Raccoon: "The Spirit of Siena"
St. Andrews Review: "The Haunted Palace," "Mosquitoes,"
   "The Bookmark"
Seneca Review: "Burning the Dolls," "The Fire Balloon"
Tar River Poetry: "Monsoon," "Certain Signs," "One Last Spider"
The World & I: "Akrotiri," "Korean Fan," "Passion Conch"

"Morpho" was reprinted in the *Anthology of Magazine Verse & Yearbook of
American Poetry,* ed. Alan F. Pater (Monitor, 1988).

I want to thank the Corporation of Yaddo for a residency, the Maryland
Arts Council for a Literary Work-in-Progress Grant, and the National
Endowment for the Arts for a Fellowship in Creative Writing.

Publication of this book is supported by grants from the National
Endowment for the Arts in Washington, D.C., a Federal agency, and
from the Pennsylvania Council on the Arts.

Contents

I

II

III

IV

for Robin
& in memory of John Logan

I was born on a street named Joy
of which I remember nothing,
but since I was a boy
I've looked for its lost turning.

> — *John Logan*
> *"Lines on His Birthday"*

I

Horse

The first horse I ever saw
    was hauling a wagon stacked with furniture
        past storefronts along Knickerbocker Avenue.
He was taller than a car, blue-black with flies,

and bits of green ribbon tied to his mane
    bounced near his caked and rheumy eyes.
        I had seen horses in books before, but
this horse shimmered in the Brooklyn noon.

I could hear his hooves strike the tar,
    the colossal nostrils snort back the heat,
        and breathe his inexorable, dung-tinged fume.
Under the enormous belly, his ——

swung like the policeman's nightstick,
    a divining rod, longer than my arm —
        even the Catholic girls could see it
hung there like a rubber spigot.

When he let loose, the steaming street
    flowed with frothy, spattering urine.
        And when he stopped to let the junkman
toss a tabletop onto the wagonbed,

I worked behind his triangular head
    to touch his foreleg above the knee,
        the muscle jerking the mat of hair.
Horse, I remember thinking,

four years old and standing there,
    struck momentarily dumb,
        while the power gathered in his thigh
surged like language into my thumb.

Reading Dickens

Not long after the war, my father
    bought, by mail, the complete set
        of the works of Charles Dickens,

each book bound in black and red
    imitation leather, the titles
        embossed in gold.

The set filled a small bookcase
    near an overstuffed chair
        where my father spent

languid evenings in lamplight,
    feet propped on the hassock,
        while David Copperfield

and honest Nicholas Nickleby
    fought their unsure way
        through a wicked world.

He might have imagined me,
    his only son, not yet born,
        on his lap, learning to read.

Each time he finished a book,
    he slipped a dollar
        between the gilt-edged pages —

some nights, the money low,
    he and my mother bounced
        before the bookcase, shaking

each volume, the few bills
    falling, enough for dinner
        or the double feature.

Decades later, reading Dickens,
    I imagine those early years,
        their slow stroll home,

her arm circling his waist,
    the whistling, papery leaves,
        the bath she drew before bed

while he waited downstairs, reading
    Dickens, happy not to be
        living some great adventure,

happy to close the book
    before my mother slept,
        saving the ending for tomorrow.

Lipstick

Who can hurry past the five-and-dime,
the cardboard Max Factor ad

fading in the yellow light
of the abandoned, fly-littered window,

without recognizing the miniature skyline —
spires, smokestacks, the blinking, red antennae —

his mother's lipsticks etched
on the powdered, greenhouse air of her bedroom?

Only God or someone taller could count them!
I wanted to explore that foreign city,

hold her hand across the cinnabar avenues,
whisper in libraries of peach frost and ruby.

Grey school-mornings in the railroad flat,
pretending to be still asleep,

I'd watch my mother dress
for the subway ride into Manhattan.

She'd sit in her bra and half-slip,
elbows propped on the vanity top,

brushing the flames across her lips,
first one flavor, then another —

forbidden strawberry, crushed orange, cafe au lait —
then close her lips on a tissue.

I'd steal the paper from the wicker
basket to taste the exotic

spices, the delicious
mocha, creme caramel, glazed papaya,

and when I was older, ten or twelve,
I'd wrap tissue after tissue

around my small, preening member,
smudging the lipstick on my flesh.

I never wrestled any desire
to smear the lipstick on my face,

touch the tubes
to my own parched lips,

but was touched by the story of Rilke,
poor Rainer, whose suffocating mother

painted the lips of her dear Maria!
O the poems! His problems with women!

Was his mother drawing out,
as she layered shade upon shade,

the lovely woman who lived inside him,
or was she blotting out,

dyeing his lips a deeper red, deeper
till almost black,

the boy who peeked
from behind his eyelids, feverish and weak?

Brooklyn Waterfall

for Stephen Dunn

Water where you least expect it:
    swelling every closet,
        tumbling down stairwells,

raining through light
    fixtures onto night tables . . .
        my good aunt Beatrice,

ever forgetful, had twisted
    the faucet handle fully,
        plugging the drain

with a red rubber stopper,
    then set off to shop.
        If water can be joyous,

imagine the unfettered
    revelry: no one home,
        the glorious, porcelain

plashing from the third
    story so loud, abandoned,
        anticipatory.

By the time she piddled
    Saturday morning away,
        the water had traveled

miles — no slow, molten
    flow, but unabashed
        raveling, elemental motion.

So when my aunt looked up
    from her swollen mop,
        my father stormed back out,

the water trailing him
　　to the local tavern.
　　　　He swilled it with bourbon.

How far he managed to float away
　　from his fearful, weeping family,
　　　　or for how many hours,

I don't remember, but
　　he swayed home later,
　　　　muttered *what the hell*,

and joined the communal
　　sweeping, work that keeps
　　　　a family together, water

still seeping into the earth
　　where it waits for us,
　　　　not needing forgiveness.

The Conversion of Saint Paul

In 1956 I was the shepherd boy
with nothing to offer the infant Jesus.

Kissed goodbye, I left the walk-up
in a white, ankle-length, terrycloth robe,

flailing my grandfather's wooden cane
wrapped from crook to tip in foil.

Secretaries stared from passing buses
at this Biblical apparition

leading his invisible sheep to school,
O little, wild-eyed prophet of Brooklyn!

Older, I portrayed the leper
gifted with half of St. Martin's cloak

and, with paper arrows and red play-dough,
evoked the passion of St. Sebastian.

Then I had to fake a terrible fall
to honor the conversion of St. Paul —

when I changed into costume
in the boys' musty coatroom,

Sister Euphrasia knelt to hike
the elastic waistband of my briefs

to better arrange my torn-sheet toga.
In second grade, this ageless ogre

had pasted Easter seals on my skull
and locked me in a cobwebbed cubicle,

pretending to air-mail me to China
where I'd never again see my mother!

Funny enough today, I guess,
but then I pleaded for forgiveness.

Now her sour breath flushed my face
when — classmates clamoring their impatience —

she whispered Jesus
would be judging my performance,

then thrust me from her failing sight
to be apprehended by all that light.

Deadly Nightshade

No friends would believe me, doubting
or jealous, and who could blame them? —
the older girls had coaxed me
into their bathroom in the bowling alley,
then dragged me into a stall
and undid the buttons of their blouses
to taunt me with black bras.

The Deadly Nightshade: their initiation,
no giggling, the moment serious
— especially for breathless Michael! —
until the burly matron stormed in
and, suddenly spooked, they bolted,
leaving me in that foreign land —
still Ridgewood Lanes, but not the same.

I dream them still, their pointy breasts,
hair bee-hived above mascara,
Luckys stuck to their lips like leeches,
all of us squeezed into the stall
while the narrow lanes outside exploded:
the thunder of whirling balls, the struck pins,
the universe shaking on its foundations.

The Haunted Palace

"If only he were young again,
he'd like to do it in a wheatfield, always."
— Cesare Pavese, "Instinct"

Some men (— women too) have told me,
without shame, about their lovemaking

in public places, how their loving
was not hurried, or self-conscious,

and the sun touching their flesh
felt good — the world made fresh!

When I was younger, nineteen or twenty,
hot-blooded and a little crazy,

I wanted to do it all the time,
no matter where: the employees'

parking-lot at lunchtime, foremen
slipping Chevys into personal slots;

the slender, Episcopal bell-tower
while the clapper tolled the hour;

the melting snowbanks on the lawn
of my parents' sullen, suburban home.

How fortunate I must have been
to find so many willing women! —

Gail Ratigan   Lucy Bamburger
Carrelia Falconi   Jennifer Foxx

Don't expect me to change their names!
We played such hoary, sensual games.

Once Bam Bam and I couldn't stop ourselves
in the slashed, graffitied cars

that wound through The Haunted Palace —
the silky, web-like streamers

caressing our cheeks, swollen
skulls blowing sheaths of tropical air,

the fluorescent doors banging open
one by one and we couldn't know

which door might break onto light,
teenagers hawking Italian ices,

surges of foam dousing the boardwalk
as we rolled and jolted and crashed

in those salt-slick recesses
where the flickering ghosts still moan

at the perfect irony of being
unable to tell what they've seen.

Small Song

for DS

I knew a woman, lovely in her bones,
Roethke wrote,
                    but the woman I knew
sheltered a stick in her womb
unlike any other bone in the body,

scrimshawed slightly
and sheathed in a hood of hair.
Three decades it tugged her attention there
till a doctor withdrew the cry from her side.

It might have been her unborn twin,
that narrow smear,
                    sweep of primal tide,
a web of blood like the candled egg's,
a mote of marrow, petrified.

Now her ache is doubly deep
with the dream of a sister twice taken,
and sleep's a music combing through her —
a lullaby, distant, singular.

Foundling

girl with marsh fever, 1824

I was born in the mouth of a bull,
my sisters tell me. I see him now,
an immense, black presence, commanding
the lilies of his field, the littlest blooms
swaying with awe among the ragged grasses.
His eye is large and liquid, the world
rounded there, and kept distant.
His lip is thick as the bow of a boat.
When I have been kissed goodnight,
the scarlet kerchief knotting my throat,
my family whispering near the fire,
I can recall the flax of his tongue,
the hand-me-down bunting of his breath,
the crooked slats of teeth: my crib.
My father was seeding furrows
when an infant's cry shrilled forth,
a song of innocence. Steaming nostrils.
And I was taken from that paludal hutch.
I was born in the mouth of a bull,
a fragile, extraordinary girl —
some ancient book holds a prophecy
I must be meant to fulfill.

Burning the Dolls

In 1851, in John Humphrey Noyes' free-love settlement in Oneida, New York, the communally-raised children, encouraged by the adults, voted to burn their dolls as representative of the traditional role of motherhood.

That last night, unable to sleep,
    I prayed with my doll
        under the twisted-star
quilt, then held her close,

her flannel gown warming my cheek,
    her hair made of yarn
        brushing the tears away.
I sang her favorite lullaby,

then she sang it back to me.
    When the sky flared into dawn
        I carried her in my arm —
not crying now for anyone to see —

to my sisters barefoot on the lawn,
    circling the stacked wood, each
        bearing some small body
that stared into the remote sun.

And when the burning was done,
    when her white, Sunday dress
        was transformed to ash
and each perfect, grasping

finger melted upon the coals,
    when her varnished face burst
        in the furnace of my soul,
the waxy lips forever lost,

then I knew I'd no longer pray,
     even with fire haunting me,
         because I hadn't resembled
closely enough my mother,

hadn't withheld my burgeoning
     desire, so like a doll
         concealing what I'd learned
I burned and burned and burned.

II

The Lighthouse Keeper at Sparrow Point

1

From the widow's walk,
he can see rows of headlights
      flaring, illuminating
the salt-struck avenues of the suburbs.

At dusk the water is gray, metallic, fringed with rust.

He'd found the journal in the supply room
among spare tubes for the radio,
coils of copper wire.

January 1, 1934
The dissolving light is shot with wind.

He pauses here, pipe-smoke drifting,
to follow with his finger
a solitary tanker running from Newport News,
low in the water, as black at this hour
as the shifting pools of oil she hauls.

He thumbs the journal slowly, imagining
the loneliness of the lighthouse keeper
who scrawled at least a sentence each dusk
for almost twenty-six years.

                    *

Half-an-hour ago he powered the generator —
the lantern began its slow,
routine blinking across the Chesapeake,
across fine networks of foam, scaffoldings of spray,
the Giacometti-like figures —
                        woman, dog, bicycle —
the wind resurrects on water,
lets travel a moment, then
plunges into black, elemental shapelessness.

                    *

Near midnight he watches the traffic
thin to a few late stragglers
returning from a holiday at the shore,
and imagines himself a boy
awakening on a back seat, staring
through fogged glass at the cone of light
throbbing the sky, to ask:
"What's that light on the water?"

His parents, talking low in front,
pause now, each wondering
what story the other might tell,
till his father, face
submerged in the green
glow of the dashboard, answers,
"The lighthouse — the Sparrow Point lighthouse."

                    *

But the boy is already drifting
back to sleep, swimming
through black water, among ghostly ice-floes,
toward the shoal, toward
the keeper of the lighthouse
silhouetted against the beacon's glare,
filled with the solitary pleasure
of watching over his family, their journey,

from slightly above this planet.

2

I'm human interest,
he thinks, coffee steaming
the lenses of binoculars, the face
of the compass, leaving
a ring on the notebook's torn cover.

He's reading the Sunday papers,
several weeks old now,
a story celebrating
"the last of the manned screwpile-design lighthouses."

I'm the man, he thinks, opening
the notebook again, skimming seasons
of faithful observation, clumsy sonnets,
starry addresses to the Lord,
the labor of an inarticulate man
hoping to explain . . .

          *

Owen Madden, lighthouse keeper, 1934–1959,
his tombstone inscribed
A Heart once Pregnant with Celestial Fire

William Pusey, 1959–1974, struck
during the worst ice-storm of the century, heart
failing like the light
before the Coast Guard managed to dock.

          *

He reads his own name in newsprint, begins
to scratch in the journal:
                    January 1, 1984
At dusk the water is gray, metallic, fringed with rust.
The dissolving light . . .

                    he pauses.

What does he have to say about light —
the everlasting eloquence
of the beacon revolving above him —

that hasn't already been spoken?

III

Snakes

for Mary Oliver

Knowing nothing about snakes, I fear them all —

the blunt, thumb-thick, foot-long diamondbacks
that idle in dry brush, motionless, for hours;

the sleek, sensual, black-eyed green snakes
that skate across the trail, then loop
around a vine, becoming the vine;

the flexuous, longer-than-I-am boa constrictors
that loll in swamp grass, gross,
rounded with a suckling
pig.

I have seen these snakes dead, hanging
full-length from a limb, being skinned
to be sold at the market in Limón.

I have seen them in my dreams, falling
from palm fronds, from rafters, from the sky.

Knowing nothing about snakes, I give them
their expanse, turn back on the narrow,
poorly-lit paths.

Ricardo, twice bitten, has given warning:
"A venomous snake will mate with a green . . .
what the guidebooks tell you is harmless
might kill you."
                              I turn away. I go back.

Knowing nothing about so many things,
I try to distinguish what's harmless
from what's not, who to be kind to,
where generosity lies.

But nothing should be ignored, nothing

doesn't matter, and even the common garter
sunning on a flat rock
can easily overwhelm us.

Costa Rica

The Spirit of Siena

> *"In certain moods, no man can weigh this world
> without throwing in something, somehow like
> Original Sin, to strike the uneven balance."*
> — Herman Melville

Wandering among the naves
like any naive tourist,
hoping to bathe in the momentary

spray of light through glass
stained with the Stations of the Cross,
I come instead face-to-face

with the crumbling, pumpkin-like head
of the centuries-dead
Catherine of Siena.

*

*Centuries dead,
I have grown tired of gazing
at improvident pilgrims like you,
the wasting-away women in black
who plead for their desperate daughters,
their sons who have fled the village
to hustle queers in harbor bars.*

*I grow so tired of their prayer,
rosaries rattling like rain,
and try to avoid their resounding
stare, but my eyelids
have withered to webs, the long
lashes scattered among eaves,
nests for generations of pigeons,
and my lips have slipped into the earth
to mate with their cousins, the worms.*

And I would like to join them
in the red dust sifting
through fingers of summer
archeologists, those who hoard the past
till only the torn
spirit is left, dwindling in the sirocco.

The world for which I suffered
virginity now tires me.
Let me lie in the light
bowl of my skull
and remember the fountain of roses
blooming where I fell.

*

Catherine of Siena, ancient
nurse wearing your habit of air,
I have wandered into your nave
as a poor man searches a pocket

of his pants draped on the bedpost,
hoping to attend the day
with some degree of faith,
a coin to close within the fist

to strike the uneven balance
in this slowly crumbling world.

*

When the severe, spoken light of God
drives its yellow
spike into the broken
marble through a crack in the dome,

the tour bus grumbles in the lot,
bleats like a startled goat
for her scattered kids.

I bid goodbye to the bodiless
woman who battled lust,
goodbye to the fat priest
mopping the altar,
a few rags bundled to his knees.

Goodbye to each flaring dust-mote
that insists itself from the shade
only to tremble away, exhausted.

And I leave behind
a few tarnished coins and this prayer
to hasten the terrible work of the air.

Mosquitoes

Last night the mosquitoes
        rose from their brackish
                beds, their mist-lit
                        mansions in the marsh,

to pour their bitter
        solutions in my ear.
                Hours I lay awake
                        listening to the wretched

soliloquies, slapping
        my breast and throat,
                snatching the air,
                        making a fist against

all I couldn't see.
        Next to me, breath
                moist and yeasty,
                        you shurred a name,

some slowly exhaled
        syllable as mosquitoes
                feasted on our flesh.
                        I lay awake, swamped

with sadness, hoping
        to shut my ears
                to their sinister
                        whisperings, malicious

fortune-tellings, those
        bearers of impossible
                bills, seedy lawyers
                        laden with subpoenas.

When the light shattered
    enough to expose them,
        four or six shadowing
            the familiar, white-

washed bricks, I raised
    my arms — *clap!* —
        miniature map of blood
            clotting my palms.

Clap! — then another.
    And as the sun calmed
        all helpless creatures
            suffering their desires,

as you stirred toward day,
    I lay awake, still,
        learning to bear
            our bitterness,

to applaud our flawed
    selves, to praise
        the words we withheld,
            blood staining my hands.

Monsoon

Rain falling so hard
you can't see through it.
Walls of slate. Slate ceiling.

Gray savaging the palms.
You can almost hear
the stars grinding.

We wait on the teak porch,
sipping rice whiskey.
Week flows into week.

We attempt to speak,
words slipping from our tongues
to dissolve on the mud floor.

And it never lets up.
The slate. The blank necessity.
All night nothingness nailing the door.

Koh Samui, Thailand

Keats' Lips

1

In the death mask by Gherardi,
the flesh has already fled
the formal bones of the face,
chiseled cheek and belled brow,

but the lips remain swollen,
almost pursed, what's left
of Keats' tumultuous spirit
struggling to forsake the mouth.

Keats might have been his own
best poem, transmutable as smoke,
but his lips were impassable:
"I lifted him up in my arms,"

Severn wrote, "and the phlegm
seemed boiling in his throat."
And when the body was no more
than a flask, the last vial

of blood broken in his lungs,
the sticks of foreign furniture,
encrusted linens and nightshirt,
even the door and window-frame

were taken by the police
and set aflame in the piazza
below the barren, February steps,
Bernini's marble boat

showering the air, bearing
the antique smell of Keats'
earthly possessions toward the sea
in the slow swirl of its grain.

2

His death mask lies in glass,
facing a sky the color of straw.
The fireplace in his room is shut.
Tourists throng the square

when the steep steps flower
and the light veers violet,
sift maps in Babington's Tea Room
and loiter below Keats' window.

In the hotel that night we argued,
hurt each other with words,
then made love, that blind, desperate
lovemaking born of loneliness.

Let me tell you this —
when her face flushed with orgasm,
as she briefly lost all control,
I was praying for Keats, his lips,

the language touched with fever
that bears us away from our bodies
and soothes the bruised soul,
if only for a few moments.

We rose with the clamor
of street cleaners and vendors
fronting fruit stands and flower stalls,
to find the sun still cloaked

with smoke rising off the Tiber.
Keats loved the light on his face
when he paused on the promenade,
and gathered momentary faith

when the hundred gray pigeons
began their awkward, flapping ascent
toward the gables and red tiles,
then vanished above the rooftops.

Yellow Stars

Starting on April 29, 1942, the Dutch Jews were forced to wear a yellow Star of David.

Crossing the Prinsengracht canal
   from the greengrocers' shops
      to the bookstalls and cafes,

grasping my mother's hand,
   the water below sweeping
      winter's debris to the sea,

I spotted three yellow stars
   bicycling toward me, fallen,
      I guess, from the sky.

I gazed through layers of air —
   daylight, but I could tell
      the stars were no longer there.

Later I saw yellow stars
   everywhere: on trams, swaying
      to Wagner in the park,

yellow stars trying to feel
   at home, hovering over
      little stars, their children.

But soon the stars floated
   away, puffs of smoke
      over the opening fields,

the icy blossoms of jasmine.
   Then winter again, our flowers
      gone, the stars vanished.

Where did the yellow stars go?
   Do you, like me, long to know,
      staring into the night

sky to search among the white,
thermal stars, the flaring
orange, for those few

yellow stars that returned
home, that call down now
to this strange planet:

behold us in the milky
light of creation
waiting to be born

Umbrellas With Souls

These bony men tumbling down 47th Street,
    umbrellas with souls,
must have escaped from vestibules, from ceramic
crocks slow-fired in foreign kilns.

Punched by wind, they are blown by ankle,
    wrist and collarbone,
taken by storm past the Gotham Book Mart
where wise men fish. Each helpless,

broken, wiry gesture by an umbrella
    draws more rain
into the barrels of their black coats,
off the slick oilcloth of their beards.

The air they displace reeks of whitefish,
    chicken broth, burgundy
tongues of too-sweet wine, cinders that flare
when the Talmud is shut like a cellar door.

One umbrella fingers his sidelock —
    the kosher delicatessen
fades slowly into an uncle whetting a sickle
in the beetfields outside Prague.

One bent umbrella smiles, eyes east —
    the diamond-district shatters.
There's my mother's mother hiding
a wedge of black bread in her blouse.

Oh New York in spring is miraculous,
    the blustery glare
a scythe slicing time — past and promise —
opening the air like lightning.

When umbrellas pause for traffic,
        pistols crack, bulletholes
blossom on the cheeks of schoolchildren.
When umbrellas let loose their souls,

garlic whipped by a ceiling fan,
        their gentle sisters
sing from the shtetls and the umbrellas of 47th Street
— listen! — tremble like bells in rain.

The Burden Lifters

At least you left me the green
        dial of the radio
                sending forth its watery

light as I listened
        to the all-night talk
                shows till, bored with G

spots, vigilantes, the midnight
        madness at Crazy Eddie's,
                I tuned in the gospel

station, letting Willis Pittman
        and his Burden Lifters
                undo the damage of too

much talk — their harmonies
        soared above New York,
                held back the endless

babble of traffic, reduced
        the hubbub of static
                to a hush. In the back-

ground rose the sound
        of women weeping, trudging
                to the altar to be touched

by some euphoric preacher
        for the sake of the souls
                of their junk-ridden sons.

How many phonecalls did I make,
        prayer aprons purchase
                from Reverend Ike, a host

of DJs spanning the seaboard,
        wanting someone to bless
                the hurt away, lift

my burden, let me groan,
        Lord, into the black
                telephone till dawn

eased down its light,
        gentle fingers upon
                my godforsaken shoulders?

Morpho

In his *Journey to the Jade Sea,*
"one of the world's greatest walkers," John Hillaby,
tells the story of the ebony child
raped and strangled
near an acacia tree in the bush in Kenya.
The game-warden who found her was mesmerized
by two large, blue-green, rarely seen butterflies
trembling upon her glazed, staring eyes,
opening and closing their wings.
Those butterflies were attracted to moisture,
lapping with their spiked, black tongues
the shallow lagoons of primeval water.
Hillaby doesn't specify, but they were probably
                the *Morpho* butterfly,
each lulled in the mirror of her dissolving eye.
Beauty and beauty often go hand-in-hand —
"what an attractive couple," we say —
but some beauties are too terrible to bear.
I've only seen a dead woman once
outside of the Ridgewood Funeral Parlor.
In Amsterdam I wandered into a bar
where a three-hundred-pound, nude, quite dead woman
shaded the jungle of a back-room pool table.
The club was hers, and she'd left provisions in her will
for the local populace to swill
the remaining stock in a sort of wake.
She was doused with beer
— the felt was soaked a deeper green —
and there, between her enormous thighs,
one silver-blue, scratchless, polished and buffed
                billiard ball
was blazing!
                I was hypnotized.

I think that combination was beautiful,
or was near to what we think of as beauty.
Still, I couldn't look for long.
My duty was to accept another beer
and hoist it, in her dubious honor,
remembering, in another pocket of the world,
the mutilated girl with butterflies upon her.

The Fire Balloon

in memoriam Elizabeth Bishop

The precise glimmerings of the fire balloon
mapped its aisle in the air
toward Cathedral Point, a slab
of granite slathered with green
that houses the maddening monkeys,
the nature trails tourists follow
to photograph the armadillo.

For hours I'd prepared the paper,
splicing and waxing and wiring,
then held the balloon at twilight
on the swollen verge of the coast
while the cotton ball soaked
in kerosene was kindled —
                              then let go.

The balloon unloosed its copper glow
over our whisperings on the strand,
even the jaundiced locals surprised
to see the paper rise and rise,
a thumb-print on the sky,
assuming kindred spirits
among the whorled, foreign stars . . .

then, miles later, tremble its descent
lee-side of the leaf-strewn crescent
to burst upon the phosphorus,
a dazzling display for the patient
still gazing over the Pacific,
something gorgeous to complete a traveling
brilliant, earth-bound, and specific.

The Turtles of Santa Rosa

haul their leathery, pock-marked backs
across the ribbed, black marl

like locals rocked with bundles
of tourists' bluejeans and socks.

They deposit their spongy eggs
in pockets gouged in sand,

then turn — so slowly! —
like the hands of wound-down clocks

to rest before dragging
their plosive hearts beyond the breakers.

We prowl with flashlights
and kneel near the nests

to observe the annual ritual
of these hundred-year-old reptiles.

And what can these ancient
washerwomen think of us,

strange creatures generating light,
stepping among the carapaces

while murmuring softly
at the green, instinctual mystery?

Some nights we see their children
struggling from the sands.

Half-conscious, they eye us
on miniature, toy-like oars —

could *we* be their earthly mothers? —
before rowing their way unerringly

toward the ceaseless, nurturing
ululations of the waves.

So I dedicate these words
to the turtles of Santa Rosa

who, a century from now,
on the scrawled floor of the sea,

having grown gentle and enormous,
might then remember me.

Costa Rica, 1985

IV

Well Water

The slender wire of the handle
insists itself in the fist,
the tin pail clatters
its history of consonance,

and the knotted rope
snakes round the pulsing wrist.
Naked, sleep-lulled, ambiguous,
I follow the twisting, narrow

path clumped with thistle,
clamber the loosening wall
to the cool, secluded
circumference of the well.

I release the pail upside-down
to break the stippled skin,
to allow the wakening water
slowly to seep in,

then haul, knot by knot,
the brimming pail over the rim.
Off balance, splotching the trail,
I heft home the tin pail

solid with the clarity of water,
its sweeping, blue parcel of sky
a metaphor of the mind
rehearsing its startled fluency.

Each morning I begin again,
drinking from the pail my fill
of the brassy, generative water,
the raised, resourceful syllable.

Ios, 1985

Akrotiri

We visit the house where the famous mural
depicting two boys boxing was found,

and a cache of clay jars
glazed with blue octopi,

a bathtub, a hairbrush —
these last remnants of civilization

stored millennia ago
by strata of volcanic ash that fell

only to be brushed away
and carted, now, to the thrashing sea.

The lost skyline, the olive window-frames,
the beauty buried below the cinders

are swept again by salt and light —
the kindled terraces are bare,

the avenues narrow enough
to hold you near me

as I touch your hair
and breathe your ancient name in Akrotiri.

Thira, 1985

Toward a Definition of Desire

"One wants anything of moment to be said
by the whole self in all its languages."
— Richard Wilbur

How many characters could we assume
in the harebells' turbulent bloom,
tumbled together those voluptuous
noons, the light slow and antique,
limb twining limb like swans
memorizing a lake, as we revised
the hushed language of our lovemaking?

How many vowels could we invent,
or reclaim from tribes long lost
below alluvia or ash?
                    We shifted
with the shifting shade, lending
our best selves to the seemingly
endless assonance.
                    We hummed
with vocables broken forth
by the blossoming of our bodies.
We were articulate, exhausting
each silt-rich syllable
with utterance.

How could we not begin again
to touch such lyrics into being,
let the bees swim the lilac
above our tongues, tender
our names to the echoing choir? —

this language let loose with each
stroke, each sigh, desire
like sunlight dampening
your thigh, the white
cleft of skin
where words
begin.

Vespers

Samos
for Robin

1

On an island you don't have much choice
    when the cafes shut
to allow the heat to diminish, so
    we climbed the flower-

ing path to Panagia Spiliani,
    renovated monastery,
its chapel set within a cave
    whose natural cisterns flow with water.

No fisherman's fish-eyed daughter
    was waiting there to guide us.
The floor was slick, the walls wet,
    while a rough, articulate

wind seemed to rush us
    toward the curvilinear cellar
where red candles anchored in sand
    signaled wildly for their dead.

In that room surrounded by the sea,
    in the moss-green light
dripping from the stalactite,
    we pressed our fingers to the stone

to lend our isolation shape —
    vast, chilling, impossible
for two people together to dispel
    with language, with gesture,

though we were able to suffer
    degrees lowering with each footfall,
the resinous breaths of the candles,
    the muted hosannas

the dead sang from their depths.
    The loamy exhalations of the planet
spun our tether to the lemon
    leaves flourishing above us.

And we were silent then, as
    the Lord of the Cave awakened,
and attended, among the flames,
    upon His voice.

Below the earth
    we don't have much choice.

2

That evening, at a cafe
    facing the umber
        waters of the harbor,
            this woman told a story:

how she once received a birthday
    card from her grandmother
        two days
            dead.

Should she spend the dollar?
    Does the message have meaning,
        or become more precious
            for its journey?

Of course, so
    she tucked the bill in a drawer,
        in a jewelry box there,
            a small burial,

two wings of paper
    folded as if in prayer,
        like the green hands of a woman
            below the spongy grass,

dead or alive,
    this moment that we share.

Traffic Island

1

Where the story begins:
some filthy kid
on the traffic island
at Houston and Bowery,
persistent and slight
among winos soaking sunlight,
black guys in bandanas
who pee on yesterday's
papers to wipe windshields
for loose change. She
brandishes a scraggly
bouquet to thrust
at stuck-at-the-light
motorists — I take
one rose for a dollar.
Near to her age,
I'd ask my grandmother
to read to me
that sentimental story
from *The Golden Treasury*:
the lost little girl
who sold matches in sleet
till her father,
in a passing carriage,
barely recognized
his dwindling daughter . . .
had she grown so strange,
rapping on windows,
begging, with gypsy eyes,
bored businessmen to buy?

2

And where it ends:
footsteps
up and down the stairs,
then the storm door
banging, woke me.
From my window, I caught
my father rushing
in pajamas into rain.
Grandmother, touched,
had fled her room again
to roam the blustery
streets in search
of her long-dead husband.
I slippered in the direction
of the Myrtle Ave.-Woodhaven
Blvd. intersection
where I found her:
stranded on the traffic
island, ghostly
nightgown flapping, yellow
taxi slowing, then hurrying on . . .
when I grasped her match-
stick arm, she gazed at me,
bewildered, but allowed herself
to be led from that barren
island, home to her spinning
bed. How could our family
fathom the history
flooding her head, the ancient
blood beginning to blossom?

Korean Fan

19th C

Perhaps, in your travels,
    you too have seen them,
        the women with soft,
            blue bundles

balanced on their heads,
    so many, a field
        of odd yet beautiful
            wildflowers, swaying

toward the river's slow swerve.
    Some, black-shawled,
        cloister near each other,
            bringing almost nothing

but their bamboo fans, each
    lacquered with a traditional
        tale, somehow personal,
            always sad.

And they keen, these widows,
    these teenage brides
        "abandoned-by-the-enlightened,"
            while they rinse again

the gauzy, formal gowns
    unworn now for seasons,
        bleached by sun, then
            arrange them on the low,

graceful brush-strokes of the ginkgo.
    All that is lovely in men
        will never be forgotten,
            each sheet bearing

the narrow imprint of one
        husband, each woven
                pillowcase the oval
                        watermark of a face.

These women never speak
        their particular grief,
                but, burdens cleansed,
                        simply creak their wrists,

stirring the shapeless
        air, allowing the blazing
                breeze to disperse
                        all sorrow. Like ghosts,

they idle in the dawn-swell,
        while the fans, so fragile,
                continue to issue
                        the light, the light

wind that blows a touch
        of grief, still unspoken,
                home with you, across
                        an indifferent ocean.

Passion Conch

No sun today, the rainy
    season barely begun, so
        we sleep late before

performing the instinctive,
    casual, tourists' ritual:
        combing the beach

in search of the unusual
    among the wrack and weedy
        debris. Ahead of me,

you scan the tide-
    line for what remains,
        the left-behind, the false

and glittering sapphires
    the salt's slow churning
        has tossed ashore —

and pull up a shell
    still filled with muscle,
        purple with black

stitching, the heart's
    colors, pulsing:
        Passion Conch:

slug that has journeyed
    farther than we have,
        from silences deeper

than sleep, withstood
    pressure beyond weather,
        seining the forgotten,

prophetic psalms of the sea —
        all ear, or tongue,
            or one foot

probing, till arriving
        here, in your hand,
            object of our naming:

Passion Conch: tight knot
        of spongy knowledge,
            scholar of coral

passages, blind traveller
        absorbing the world:
            salt water, green

minutiae, perhaps two lovers
        biding time in the gray
            light, in light

rain, turning their deep
        desire over and over,
            having finally found,

in the foreign face,
        in the blunt, breathing
            body, a kindred

race, the source
        of flame, a gift,
            a name.

                    Hua Hin, Thailand

Romance in the Old Folks' Home

First he offered to read to her,
but she was afraid
he spoke as Bible-thumper, so declined.

Then he steeped several
herbal teas for her table —
she sipped without looking up.

He scissored photos from weeklies
and taped them to her door,
little windows into the past:

couples skating on Highland Pond,
dancing four days in a marathon,
sleeping on roofs above Flatbush Avenue.

She knew she was being spoken to
in a language long forgotten,
like Latin lost after school.

When she found the horned shell
near her lounge on the lawn,
she pressed it to her ear

to hear the ceaseless *hush*,
knowing longing had replaced
the sluggish creature housed there.

The next evening she appeared
with freshly-washed hair
pinned with an ivory comb,

and brought that shy spirit
her favorite book —
The Marble Faun by Nathaniel Hawthorne

who liked to brood on sin —
while the faint widows flushed
and whispered her name — oh Anna! —

and she asked him please to begin.

The Bookmark

In *Page's Rhyming Dictionary*
(Boston: Talbot & Sons, 1820),

inscribed "To Her Loving Child,
Nathaniel, in His Sickness,"

between "soul" and "spirit,"
those yellow, translucent leaves,

I found a spider
crushed among the rhymes,

a bookmark from the romantic
century pressed there

by a feverish boy
while composing his own elegy.

There's no need to be
so melancholy —

we know the boy lived.
Let's say he was startled

by the report of the slammed
book, so loud so late,

then surprised with himself,
his mild joke

committed in the privacy
of a parlor gabled with snow,

during the February quarantine,
so many sicknesses ago.

Certain Signs

Like weeds along the roadside,
this proliferation of the handmade:
U-PICK-EM, white paint on wooden slabs,
so we ease the car into honeysuckle
and raise the dust of previous summers
as we carry our baskets into the patch.

I reach below the prickly cowling
to pluck ripe strawberries
flecked with dirt, the green
leaves like new money in our palms.
Once, on Covert Street, a flutter of bills
from a third-story window as we
cruised the neighborhood near midnight. . .
we shoved and screamed, greedy
kids, grubbing as much as we could —
money from the moon —
then ran home to recount
the crazy shouting above us.
                              Twelve dollars.
This will happen again, I thought.

As it is happening now, a different
currency as I stoop to this task,
strawberries plush and giving
as immigrant grandmothers, clouds
of mayflies swarming my hair,
this woman on her knees in the next row
staining her cotton dress as,
basket brimming, she piles strawberry
upon strawberry in her lap.

Later, in the light wash of evening,
the strawberries rinsed and cooled
in thick cream, I grin
as she takes the first bite, juice
overflowing her lips, her eyes
tearing with the tart,
sexual taste of gleaned
strawberries, full of this moment
no money in the known world can purchase.

One Last Spider

New year, rime on the pane,
  the upper story luminous
    with streetlight, snowlight —

line by easy line, I repeat
  this trite, page-worn
    scene, familiar

liar in a web of words,
  struggling to break through
    to something true . . .

so I think of you, asleep
  after the spontaneous
    litany of lovemaking,

the tumult of blankets, of breath.
  I left our bed pages ago,
    brushing through gummy

scaffolding a late spider
  had lashed to the lintel,
    invisible strands

tugging — as we were held,
  briefly, by the glistening
    filament of semen

as I slipped away from you.
  The gloss on your lips,
    musk on my fingertips,

the slender lines filling the air —
  this I know to be true —
    will soon fade, then disappear.

When we make love again,
    I'll desire the light
        to sketch our shadows

upon the wall, a tender
    tangle of limbs,
        one last spider

marking his slow but sure
    progress from nothing
        to a thrumming architecture.

Carnegie Mellon Poetry

1975
The Living and the Dead, Ann Hayes
In the Face of Descent, T. Alan Broughton

1976
The Week the Dirigible Came, Jay Meek
Full of Lust and Good Usage, Stephen Dunn

1977
How I Escaped from the Labyrinth and Other Poems,
   Philip Dacey
The Lady from the Dark Green Hills, Jim Hall
For Luck: Poems 1962-1977, H. L. Van Brunt
By the Wreckmaster's Cottage, Paula Rankin

1978
New & Selected Poems, James Bertolino
The Sun Fetcher, Michael Dennis Browne
A Circus of Needs, Stephen Dunn
The Crowd Inside, Elizabeth Libbey

1979
Paying Back the Sea, Philip Dow
Swimmer in the Rain, Robert Wallace
Far From Home, T. Alan Broughton
The Room Where Summer Ends, Peter Cooley
No Ordinary World, Mekeel McBride

1980
And the Man Who Was Traveling Never Got Home,
   H. L. Van Brunt
Drawing on the Walls, Jay Meek
The Yellow House on the Corner, Rita Dove
The 8-Step Grapevine, Dara Wier
The Mating Reflex, Jim Hall

1981
A Little Faith, John Skoyles
Augers, Paula Rankin
Walking Home from the Icehouse, Vern Rutsala
Work and Love, Stephen Dunn
The Rote Walker, Mark Jarman
Morocco Journal, Richard Harteis
Songs of a Returning Soul, Elizabeth Libbey

1982
The Granary, Kim R. Stafford
Calling the Dead, C. G. Hanzlicek
Dreams Before Sleep, T. Alan Broughton
Sorting It Out, Anne S. Perlman
Love Is Not a Consolation; It Is a Light, Primus St. John

1983
The Going Under of the Evening Land, Mekeel McBride
Museum, Rita Dove
Air and Salt, Eve Shelnutt
Nightseasons, Peter Cooley

1984
Falling From Stardom, Jonathan Holden
Miracle Mile, Ed Ochester
Girlfriends and Wives, Robert Wallace
Earthly Purposes, Jay Meek
Not Dancing, Stephen Dunn
The Man in the Middle, Gregory Djanikian
A Heart Out of This World, David James
All You Have in Common, Dara Wier

1985
Smoke From the Fires, Michael Dennis Browne
Full of Lust and Good Usage, Stephen Dunn (2nd edition)
Far and Away, Mark Jarman
Anniversary of the Air, Michael Waters
To the House Ghost, Paula Rankin
Midwinter Transport, Anne Bromley

1986

Seals in the Inner Harbor, Brendan Galvin
Thomas and Beulah, Rita Dove
Further Adventures With You, C. D. Wright
Fifteen to Infinity, Ruth Fainlight
False Statements, Jim Hall
When There Are No Secrets, C. G. Hanzlicek

1987

Some Gangster Pain, Gillian Conoley
Other Children, Lawrence Raab
Internal Geography, Richard Harteis
The Van Gogh Notebook, Peter Cooley
A Circus of Needs, Stephen Dunn (2nd edition)
Ruined Cities, Vern Rutsala
Places and Stories, Kim R. Stafford

1988

Preparing to Be Happy, T. Alan Broughton
Red Letter Days, Mekeel McBride
The Abandoned Country, Thomas Rabbitt
The Book of Knowledge, Dara Wier
Changing the Name to Ochester, Ed Ochester
Weaving the Sheets, Judith Root

1989

Recital in a Private Home, Eve Shelnutt
The Age of Krypton, Carol J. Pierman
Land That Wasn't Ours, David Keller
Stations, Jay Meek
The Common Summer: New and Selected Poems,
   Robert Wallace
The Burden Lifters, Michael Waters
Falling Deeply into America, Gregory Djanikian